MW00526770

Nov 9/2021

TREATY

To Ted:

Real pleasure to
meet you & chat,

Miigwech,

Also by Armand Garnet Ruffo

Poetry
Opening In the Sky
Grey Owl: The Mystery of Archie Belaney
At Geronimo's Grave
The Thunderbird Poems

Prose
Norval Morrisseau: Man Changing Into Thunderbird

Film
A Windigo Tale, feature, writer-director
Jiigishkaand, The Door, short, writer-director
On the Day the World Begins Again, short, writer

Anthologies
(Ad)Dressing Our Words: Aboriginal Perspectives on Aboriginal Literatures,
  editor
An Anthology of Canadian Native Literature in English, co-editor
An Introduction to Indigenous Literary Criticism in Canada, co-editor
An Anthology of Indigenous Literature in Canada, co-editor

TREATY

ARMAND GARNET RUFFO

XXX

A Buckrider Book

Buckrider Books is an imprint of Wolsak and Wynn Publishers.

Cover design: Robin Moon
Interior design: Marijke Friesen
Cover image: courtesy of Hugh McGoldrick
Author photograph: Pearl Pirie
Typeset in Minon Pro
Printed by Coach House Printing Company Toronto, Canada

The publisher gratefully acknowledges the support of the Canada Council for the Arts,
the Ontario Arts Council and the Government of Canada.

Buckrider Books
280 James Street North
Hamilton, ON
Canada L8R 2L3

Library and Archives Canada Cataloguing in Publication

Title: Treaty # / Armand Garnet Ruffo.
Other titles: Treaty number
Names: Ruffo, Armand Garnet, 1955- author.
Description: Poems.
Identifiers: Canadiana 20190062460 | ISBN 9781928088769 (softcover)
Classification: LCC PS8585.U514 T74 2019 | DDC C811/.54—dc23

10 9 8 7 6 5 4 3 2 1

For those ancestors who signed treaty in good faith.

And in memory of Richard Wagamese,
when we dreamed of writing books.

The poet enjoys the incomparable privilege of being able to be at once himself and someone else. – Charles Baudelaire, "Crowds"

Those who authentically commit themselves to the people must re-examine themselves constantly. – Paulo Freire, *Pedagogy of the Oppressed*

IMPETUS UNGAINLY

Doctrine of Discovery /3
The Tap /5
Pink Mints /7
The Shop /8
The Claim /9
Reckoning /10
On the Day the World Begins Again /11
A Love Story /13
Dinner Party /14
The Unsettling /16
#1: Red Space /18
#2: White Space /19
The Real Indians /20
Minobimaadizwin, The Good Life /22
Filament /24
Torque Wrench /25
Raising a Boy /26
Weetigo Memory /27
The Material World /28
Red Is a Poem /29
The Poet /31

TRAVELOGUE SIGHTLINE

Wallace Stevens's Memory /35
Carrier Woman /36
Why Don't You Write? /38
Missing /40
Lake Cousin /41
Under Construction /42
At My Great-Grandfather's Cabin /46
Artifice /47
Pauline Johnson's Dress, 1892 /48
At Père-Lachaise /50
The Zen Garden in Kyoto /51
Lluvia De Oro /53
Fireflies /54
Mississauga Golf Club /55
Hidden Residential School Graveyard /56
Haliburton Highlands Night /57
Old Warrior /58
Indian Fare /59
Terra Nullius Lingus /62

BOREAL INVESTIGATIVE

Zhawenjigewin /65
Luck /66
Biblical /67
God /69
Old House /70
Family Time /71
First Words /72
Bimodegos, Going Through the Bush in Winter /74
Birds at Dawn /75
Spider and the Sun /76
Catching Bees /77
Congregation /78
Treaty Letter /80
Sudbury, Night /82
Ethic /83
The Coming /84
Small Defiance /85
Structuralism /86
Once /88
Sentient /89
Water Lily Woman /90
Nanabozhoo /93
A Wise Man Once Told Me /94

Acknowledgements /96
Notes /97

IMPETUS UNGAINLY

Treaty No. 9

ARTICLES OF A TREATY made and concluded neewteb, evif dna derdnuh enin dna dnasuoht eno droL ruO fo raey eht ni niereht denoitnem setad lareves eht ta, between His Most Gracious Majesty the King of Great Britain, srenoissimmoC siH yb dnalerI, dnaand Duncan Campbell Scott, of Ottawa, dna eriuqsE, oiratnO, Samuel Stewart, eriuqsE, oiratnO Ontario, and Daniel George MacMartin, of Perth, Ontario, eriuqsE, eht gnitneserper fo ecnivorp Ontario, dna trap eno eht fo and the Ojibeway, Cree and other Indians, ... nemdaeh dna sfeihc, rieht yb, debircsed dna denifed retfaniereh stimil eht nihtiw territory eht fo stnatibahni.

Whereas, the Indians inhabiting the territory ot tseretni fo srettam niatrec nopu etarebiled ot 1905 fo raey tneserp siht ni yrotirret dias eht ni secalp niatrec ta Canada fo noinimoD eht fo tnemnrevog s'ytsejaM siH gnitneserper noissimmoc a teem ot denevnoc neeb evah denifed retfaniereh deliberate upon certain matters tseretni fo to His Most Gracious Majesty, fo eht one part, and the said Indians rehto eht fo.

And, whereas, the said Indians demrofni dna deifiton neeb evah by His Majesty's ecneloveneb dna ytnuob s'ytsejaM siH morf eviecer dna nopu tnuoc ot era yeht secnawolla tahw fo derussa eb dna wonk yam elpoep naidnI siH taht dna, stcejbus rehto s'ytsejaM siH dna meht neewteb good-will and peace eb yam ereht taht os meht, htiw egnarra dna ytaert a ekam ot dna, tcart dias eht gnitibahni stcejbus naidnI siH fo oterent tnesnoc eht niatbo ot dna, denoitnem retfaniereh sa debircsed dna dednuob, yrtnuoc fo tcart a teem mees yam ytsejaM siH ot sa sesoprup rehto hcus gnirebmul, gninim, levart, edart, noitargimmi, tnemelttes rof nepo ot erised siH si ti taht noissimmoc dias yb His Majesty's.

And whereas, the said commissioners a etaitogen ot dedeecorp evah treaty with the Ojibeway, Cree and other Indians, dna rednerrus, esaeler,

1

edec ybereh od snaidnI dias eht, rednuereh denoitnem setad eht ta sdnab evitcepser eht yb dedulcnoc dna, nopu deerga neeb sah emas eht dna, debircsed dna denifed retfaniereh tcirtsid eht gnitibahni yield up to the government of the Dominion of Canada, rof siH Majesty the King and His na gniniatnoc dnal dias eht 3 .oN ytaerT elgnA tsewhtroN eht yb dedec yrotirret eht fo yradnuob nretsae eht fo trap a yb tsew eht no dna wal, yb denifed sa oiratnO fo ecnivorp dias eht fo seiradnuob eht yb htron dna tsae eht no dednuob dna . . . fo area of ninety thousand square miles, erom ro ssel.

And His Majesty the King hereby agrees htiw eht dias Indians taht they shall have the thgir eb emit ot emit morf yam sa snoitaluger hcus ot tcejbus, debircsed erofotereh sa derednerrus tcart eht tuohguorht gnihsif dna gnipparт, gnitnuh fo snoitacov lausu rieht eusrup ot eht yb edam government of the yrtnuoc.

His Majesty, raey txen taht seerga osla and annually afterwards for ever, . . . ereht sselnu, emas eht srallod ruof deifiton yluf eb llahs snaidnI dias eht hcihw fo setad dna secalp elbatius ta hsac ni snaidnI dias eht ot diap eb ot esuac lliw eh.

Witnesses:

THOMAS CLOUSTON RAE, C.T.,   DUNCAN CAMPBELL SCOTT.
Hudsons Bay Co.   SAMUEL STEWART.
ALEX. GEORGE MEINDL, M.D.   DANIEL GEORGE MACMARTIN
JABEZ WILLIAMS, Commis,   MISSABAY, his x mark
H. B. Co.   THOMAS his x mark MISSABAY . . .
    [What does x mean anyway?]

Doctrine of Discovery

The ants enter the room
bodies glazed in black armour.
They march down the walls
and across the desk.
I can see they are on a mission
held to some master plan
a doctrine of discovery.

When I slap them with my hand
target them with my finger
poke them with my pen
they ignore me
as though everything
were for the taking.
It's getting so I'm beginning
to think I am living a never-
ending nightmare

It's like they are trying
to bore themselves into me
plant themselves
into my brain.
Last night one of them
landed on my head
and I awoke with a start.
When I turned on the light
it scurried under my pillow.

I stomp on them
but they keep coming
day after day after day.
And I'm beginning to think

it is a hopeless war
I've waged. I stomp
and stomp and new recruits
arrive to fill their ranks.
Their determination
is collective mania.

Though I've sealed the doors
and the windows
they keep coming.
And I am beginning to think
they are looking for something
to take in their pincers
and devour, something
supreme like God
like Creation itself
as they carry
the dead away.

The Tap

My mind is a town with main street looking like it's had its teeth punched
in. Broken windows and empty lots. And then, it's a bright Saturday
morning, and I'm riding my bike down to the beach.

My parents relax on creaky lawn chairs.
I can hear their every move. They are in the shade
of a house made of bone and tarpaper.

My sister is screaming the house is on fire. We run
to the Japanese neighbours. Exiles like us, my mother whispers.
In their tiny kitchen, we drink cocoa where everybody is safe.

My aunt is in a western bar dancing. She throws her cowboy hat
in the air, revealing her bald head. Everyone turns away except me.
Then my sister says she's doesn't want to die, but she dies anyway.

I am ten again. We go for a family picnic, and I get carsick.
The dust from the road in my hair, clothes, mouth. When we arrive
I jump into a lake, and find I can't swim. My father drags me out.

When we return a neighbour is skinning a bear on his back porch,
something he does regularly. The bear is staring at me.
His eyes get bigger and bigger, until they become moons.

I arrive at a friend's door just in time to overhear him say
I don't believe in sin. His parents tell him I'm just a little pagan.
I try to creep away, but the floorboards thunder with every footstep.

At home my dog Chopper is smiling at me with a curled lip, and
I am loving him in a moment so perfect the world opens for me. The
moment is a silver hook cast into a bottomless lake. Floating until it sinks.

It's true. Some memories cannot be turned off with sleep. I jolt awake, go for a glass of water, pull the curtains aside. The light in the yard beside the tree is hard yellow. The dripping tap punctuates the night.

Pink Mints

They're in the kitchen laughing. I'm on the couch half watching the hockey game. Saturday night, and Mervin is making up my mother. He applies some red lipstick and digs into his black case and takes out a small paintbrush. He dips it into a small container and brushes her cheeks. My mother is wearing her sparkly blue dress and black high heels that match her black hair. Mervin's wearing a tight white shirt, yellow socks, pointed shoes and black slacks, the dress-up kind I wear on special occasions.

When I was younger Mervin used to babysit me and other kids from the neighbourhood. He'd take us to the movie theatre where he'd give us brooms we'd push around like a little army. He'd let us keep any money we found, and we'd stick our thin arms between the seats feeling for coins. If we behaved ourselves, at the end of the job he'd stick his arm behind the locked candy counter and slip out a package of mints.

He always grabbed the pink ones. We preferred them anyways. The white ones burned our mouths. We'd stand in a row, and Mervin would drop a mint on our tongues just like Communion. Tonight they're going to The Sportsman's Lounge or maybe to a party. I tell them to have a good time, go back to the hockey game and don't think anything. That will come later from the snickers of the kids at school. Where I'll float above myself and act like I don't know him.

The Shop

The engines buckle and crash as my tiny hands shoot up over my ears.
How big the world looks when there are ten engines in a row rumbling
in their dragon lair. Tamed by mechanics who shout and wave me away
over the deafening. But they are too busy to bother with me.
This place, it is like having the power of diesel in your belly, every
limb shaking. Even though there are signs posted everywhere that say
this is private property, trespassers will be prosecuted, I come anyway.

In mid-winter, thirty below, this is my route to school. Cautiously I cut
through the shop, stopping momentarily at the steaming radiators for
warmth. In the summer when the climate sweats, it is reverse in here,
the stone walls bleed coolness. Old man Frown lives down the road
and when I spot him in his oily overalls I beat it for the heavy doors.
I'm afraid of him and run as fast as I can, because sometimes his wife
comes to see my mother with her eyes nearly swollen shut. She asks me
to go to the drugstore for her.

The Claim

January. So cold the Odawa Native Friendship Centre van
scours the streets and alleys for the homeless in a land
that is home. The irony is not lost in the pitch of night
when the house groans and creaks above the frozen earth –

human, sentient, cognizant, tough, pitiless –
while my young son wheezes from a chest cold.
I turn up the heat and the furnace kicks in blowing
heat up through tropical philodendra. There was a time

when I would have stoked a wood stove, stuffed out wind
from boxcar walls, us kids wearing sweaters and socks to bed,
unthawing our hands in whatever water was left on the stove.
But that was another life and just yesterday my neighbour

looked me in the eye and told me I've done well for myself,
as though announcing the second coming of Christ. I didn't
say anything, although I guess I should have. You see those
who really know know for each gain there is a loss, an accounting,

a claim. I see ghosts of family through the curtains smiling
at me, in sunshine, in a forest, bathing in a small lake
holding all the warmth of summer, they are speaking
to me in a language I don't understand.

Reckoning

#1

Listen! you may believe it merely story: but once we glistened
like a bird's golden plumage, our bodies all we had to offer up,
our humanity, everlasting truth be told, the great unravelling unravelled
one dull morning, clocked in, perpetually beaten, self-medicated,
incapacitated, picture some dung beetle in the muck of it, volition /
violation, volatile / velocity, we rolled out of bed into the numbing
unacknowledged, unaccounted, paralyzed spine of less-than

#2

Listen! that thing you drove over, that collision of histories leaves us all
crawling in this ethereal city where once came to a reverberating halt
under the steady gaze of sexy prophets, shiny gods, fast cars, fast food,
clear cut, clear conscience, half-life, half-lie, while the patriotic and
ordinary citoyen rush about doing ordinary things like washing face
and hands or letting them go dirty, get filthy

#3

Listen! you may prefer to be strung along like a fish underwater but here
is water at your feet and rising, you see that thing was me, damn it,
and is me, stoked and stroked by transitory belonging, high resolution
flat words, like *happiness* and *reconciliation*, but there is no two ways,
no fear, it is too late for that the earth will heal herself, eventually,
magnificently, when our species is gone the way of the last redwood,
that looks with its cedar eyes across the belly of America, to this
naked World, witness to the inevitable reckoning

On the Day the World Begins Again

On the day the world begins again
will it be the strongest animal
the swiftest bird
or the tiniest insect
that carries the news to humankind
announces rebirth in a roar
in a squeak or maybe in silence?

On the day the world begins again
will luminous light
rise from parting clouds
in unquestionable power
and refract a miraculous prism of colour
while the tallest white pine announces peace
in a sprinkling of communion?

On the day the world begins again
will those suspended behind bars
in and between grey ugliness
in their deadened shouts of protest
float beyond their circle of cigarette burns
and crude tattoos
beyond their sharp cries of where
they are and wish they were?

On the day the world begins again
will their re/imagined selves
the shape of thought
the shape of prayer
bend like molten steel
in the fire at the centre of the human heart
Will they rise beyond themselves
and find their way home
On the day the world begins again
will the cages open for them?

A Love Story

When he was young he met a girl who told him she was Jewish. He told
her he was lost, and she fell in love with him, and he with her. No one
had ever loved him like her before. No one had ever loved her like him.
For a while he saw flowers bloom in slow motion. She saw sunlight and
afternoon showers watering those same flowers. What they didn't know
is that they both carried scars as deep as the world, a place where flowers
don't grow. One day he walked in and tears were streaming down her
cheeks like a river and he knelt beside her and cupped his hands. He was
familiar with tears. As a baby he had bathed in them. The television was
on, and he saw she had been watching a movie about WW II. One day she
came in, and he had a shard of a beer bottle in his hand. He was trying to
cut out a place for himself in the world. She could see he had been watching
a western. She told him it was just a movie just as he had told her it was just
a movie. The thing is they both innately understood it wasn't just a movie.
It was the world. It was like when they made love and searched each other's
bodies for healing, but being young, their bodies perfect for each other,
the scars were invisible. They were in fact so perfect they blindly ignored
them and naively thought they would fade (into the sunset?). That was not
the case. The more they loved, the more their hurt twisted and ached for
understanding, for enduring, binding them to their pain, until all we could
do was not love.

Dinner Party

Substratum of living
room conversation
pleasant company
books and a fireplace,
safe and almost in
the affairs of the day:
gender, war, politics,
reconciliation, tv

a fractured shift
and a shadow jack pine
scrapes its perpetual
one-pitch note against
a single-pane window
as a dinner plate zings
and shatters, a white
towel soaks up blood,
and what was that?

another shift of head
and our gracious host
stands before us
announcing it's time,
everyone rising on cue
like the sumptuous aroma
into a setting for six,
candles and fine china,
brimming anticipation

while steps away a fault line
you take heed to step across:
temporal simulacrum
precambrian rock-cut
arboreal town
precarious shack
deceptive home
leaking shadow
across easy smiles

The Unsettling

On this rez nobody says anything

they haven't talked in a century
this is how it happens:
a girl (fourteen) is raped
a neighbour (twenty-one) is charged
he is already alcoholic
his father is absent
his mother looks for excuses
she was thrown into ugliness
(ugly school, ugly loneliness, ugly walls, ugly
cold, ugly food, ugly fists, ugly you get the picture)
she has never climbed out

the girl's uncle is a rez cop
he says we can't change the past
but it is our responsibility
to change the future –
I ask what does that mean exactly?
I guess he should know
he tells me stories that make me want
to bang my head against the wall
he lives this stuff daily
he was born out of its chaos

but really, don't kid yourself
everyone knows the magnitude
you have heard the stats:
for every Indian who graduates
from high school
ten Indians end up in jail
the only difference now
is a few are starting to speak
she says she will confront him

am I saying too much?

#1: Red Space

accolades gather upon her – And she sits nearby on clouds
she wears them proudly – Holding a rainbow in her hands
highlighting her grey hair – There is so much to consider when I consider
against her shining skin – Her light, I see sunlight
i can tell she is wise – Not honey, gold, silk, fine china wise, not that
when we meet she smiles – And there I am painted in the background
radiantly in a room of devotees – Maybe you are one of them?
though later alone with me – That's okay, I understand now
she is not shy to judge and – What? Of course this is only my interpretation
condemn *those* white Indians – the kind who'd never make it in Hollywood
i don't say a word, stay silent – I was always the introverted type anyway
like the ghost she turns me into – Always
what I could say is I became – Became what? Became human?
at around six – Ha, I know what you are going to say
when a kid at school – Turned on me. In hindsight you have to wonder why
told me with a sneer – Can you say it in Anishinaabemowin?
my mother – Did I tell her? Honestly, I don't remember
was a squaw – There it is. Launched to explode-implode
or maybe it was – Me, I was turned into shame, I shrank
a few years later – A lifetime. I'm sure you can see that by now
when I had a valentine – Handmade, I'd spent the day cutting and pasting
returned to me – Why? Did I innately know why?
because nobody – I sat at the back of the class with the other misfitted
wants one – My beautiful handmade card
from an – Don't say it. Don't say it. Don't say it
indian – There it is. I said it. If you sneer it sounds like squaw
at least that's what he – I wonder how he felt about it?
her brother – I wonder who put him up to it?
told me – I never did ask her ☹

#2: White Space

She asks me why I write *influenced* – aren't we all?
by my Ojibwe heritage – from the beginning I confess
and not simply am – to be or not to be, is anything ever simple?
I say, my white space – I remember standing in front of a mirror
goes back to the 1700s – not that far back for sure, maybe I was six
when a Spanish navigator – something romantic about this
working for the British – you know, no shame there
jumped ship. Ever wonder – a wanted man
why way up in northern Ontario – rivers
there's an Espanola – have you been? not much there, rivers & Indians
a Spanish River? – as a kid I watched the canoeists leaving from Biscotasing
So the story goes – my grandmother told this with a giggle
he fell in love – maybe it made her proud, did that take a while too?
and nine months later – us
so there you have it – couldn't put it any plainer
You see, it's something – I hate explaining
people who aren't – aren't what?
really comfortable – who is?
in their skin – the colonized, Fanon
they might pretend to be – wear braids, wear a name, that kind of thing,
but believe me – who's kidding who?
(I clear my throat at this point – blank)
they feel the slings – oh, poor pitiful me, I love Ronstadt singing it
and arrows – love Shakespeare too & he's a Brit
tend to do. Oh – another confession coming up
and Giovanni Caboto – putting it all on the table
(a.k.a. John Cabot – blank)
landed here in 1497 – back in the day
Ha! – I actually visited Castello Ruffo ☺

The Real Indians

#1

When I asked my sister why Grandma refused to talk about the fathers of
her children, the two men who walked out on her leaving her to fend for
herself, she looked hard at me because I was a man and it went without
saying I wouldn't understand. After all, it was my kind who were the root
of the problem. Once in a restaurant I pressed her to explain, and she got
up and walked out and left me sitting at the dinner table alone.

#2

The real Indians weren't like us Grandma used to say staring off into
space, though she spoke fluent Ojibwemowin and grew up in the bush.
The real Indians stayed out on the horizon. A paddle in the air to wave
a greeting. They never approached. They didn't want the white man's
disease. They didn't want anything to do with the white man.

#3

When she was younger Grandma moved to Toronto to work in the
garment industry. Like many Indigenous people, she grew up sewing,
and she used her skill as a way to survive. Her two daughters stayed
in the village with their grandparents, and she travelled to see them
when she could. She liked working for her Jewish boss, and she was
proud of the work she did for him.

#4

The real Indians only went to the HBC post when it was absolutely necessary. They lived off the land, hunted deer and moose, packed blueberries into neat birchbark baskets so thick you could slice the berries with a knife. The life they lived was rich, and they had the best of everything the bush could offer. They wanted for nothing.

#5

When she was middle-aged she was back in the north country (as she called her home) and met an older trapper and married him. Her dreams of having a real husband had finally come true. He gave her a son but died soon thereafter. She spoke about this man, the love of her life, for the rest of her life.

#6

The real Indians watched the stars and told stories, Aadizookaan, as old as the stars. Of Nanabozhoo whose father is the West Wind. The real Indians never saw a beer parlour. Or a bingo hall. Or a television. Never saw a school of any kind. They never moved to reserves. Or towns. Or cities. Never even moved to Canada.

#7

I was visiting her at the Aboriginal Wigwamen residence in Toronto, where she had moved to be close to her children. I had showed up with a bar stool for her because she had a tall counter in the kitchen, and that's when she first told me about the real Indians. A fragment my grandmother longed for, elaborated upon as she got older and older and saw what had become of her people on Spadina Avenue, and maybe what had become
of herself.

Minobimaadizwin, The Good Life

When he was young with stars and maps in his eyes
he found himself in Tuscany on a hillside garden   (if this
tending sheep. His journey took him through   sounds
the narrow medinas of Marrakech, across the   idyllic
desert to orange groves in Algiers, bread   for the
in clay ovens, to cafe sweets in Tunis,   young
over a stormy Mediterranean where Aegaeon   it
or Poseidon or maybe Neptune caught him   is)
sleeping on deck one night and tried to
sweep him into the sea, but he held on
to the good life.

All that was before

he got home and saw first-hand that not everyone
gets out or in. There was a little girl you see   is it
with hair like night sitting cold in a doorway   idyllic
on a rough wood floor, a T-shirt in sub-zero   this
weather, snot dripping from her nose. This   sound(s)
was Canada, and he was home on Native land.   for the
Shoot ahead forty years, and the radio blasts   young
that a young Cree girl hung herself   this
in a closet in Attawapiskat, in muskeg   is it
and black spruce, a community so remote and
out of mind it's not even on a road map.

Oh Canada, to be young and not suicidal. Free
to ride the waves of Hudson Bay or the
Mediterranean, to nearly get washed out to sea.
But not quite, thanks to your Manitous, your
Nanabozhoo, your Weesageechak, your
determination to hold on. What is that thing
that makes it so for some and not for others?
Politicians are quick to tweet education, health
care, gainful employment, factories, shopping
malls, income supplements as if they were iron
pills. But we know what the cure is, we have known
it forever, Aabanaabi' izhi mikaniyan o'ow wanisin.[1]

this
this
is it
for the
young
(sounds
idyllic
if
it is)

---

1 S/he looks back in a certain way to find what is lost.

Filament

Always that spectral fragment. Filament of line cast back there.
Where open-mouthed fish rise to gulp down shiny lures.

I sang once in an auditorium to almost empty rows.
I looked for my people in the seats, under the seats, behind
the seats, but they weren't there. I called the three people
who were there to come up and introduce themselves.
They were young aspirants. They talked about themselves
their professional websites. They talked about their astronomical
aspirations. What they didn't talk about is why.

Maajaa. Time collapses everything. Origami people.
We're all eventually blown away into uncertainty.

Azhegiiwe. Is that how you say it? It's that too.
We all return, if only by the stars.

For a while we thought we could change the world.
For a while we thought we had a place in the world.

The offers came. Good ones. Corner offices. Security.
Mortgages. Investments. Cars. Boats. Houses. Memberships
to health clubs, fan clubs. Promotion. Seduction. Reduction.
Fame. Fame. Fame.
He says, business is business. She says, look at me.
I say, it was planned and bound to happen.

Together we held the thrashing fish in our hands and felt the world slip.

Torque Wrench

Confused and frightened world, addendum: what
is going on? where is it? is it lost? what is going on?
missing and murdered women, mass murder everyday
last year in the USA – 365 in 365 – terrorist attacks
in Paris, bombing in Burkina Faso, hotel Splendid
not so splendid, and I am nearly out of my mind
searching for my torque wrench, ½-drive,
set at 89 ft-lb, the one I need to fix the tire
survey the yard-shed-trunk-shed-yard
What's that, dad? my young son says
hearing the radio as we get ready to drive
to the grocery store, once upon a time rabbits
snared innocently by a boy for supper,
snowshoes and brass wire thin as a hair
set beside an old river he knew instinctively
would always be there even as he began to fade
What's that, dad? Instead I search for music
any music, and hum along because some days
that's all there is to feel something better

Raising a Boy

for Alex

teach him he is beginning
teach him to put his hand on his chest
teach him to take this thing he feels for his mother
teach him his mother is the earth
teach him to take it in his hand
teach him to blow on it and give it breath
teach him he is beginning
teach him it is the creator's breath
teach him he's just made the world
teach him to watch it closely as it floats above him
teach him to look at all the rivers and lakes and mountains
teach him this world can be anything
teach him he is beginning
teach him to imagine it is on fire
teach him to be careful not to burn himself
teach him many people live lives of fire
teach him they are not happy people
teach him they break things
teach him he is beginning
teach him his job is to fix things
teach him they don't know any better
teach him his job is to know better
teach him once there was a great flood
teach him it is the same flood in every culture
teach him he is beginning
teach him once the fire went out
teach him the water brought beginning
teach him the people lived in peace
teach him he is water
teach him to be happy
teach him he is beginning

Weetigo Memory

The artist jumps on stage to celebrate his achievements,
takes a moment to honour his grandfather and reads
an accented story about the Weetigo, a gaunt monster
with a greedy appetite – the gaping mouth of residential school
sucking the marrow from his grandfather's bones,
slurping his blood, exposed brain, and body and spirit
digested and regurgitated for the rest of his days. But
good times are in his words too.

He says they continue to carry him. Can they? What is swept
into the wind returns. I picture him and the old man in a half-
ton bouncing down a dusty reserve road stopping at landmarks,
half-remembered naming, Niiwak stories of family and
community in the language of a time when the earth was young
like a boy on his grandfather's knee, hands clasped together
on the steering wheel. Bad medicine, maci-maskihkiy
passed on, unnoticed, pulsing red.

The Material World

Oh, my poor sick neighbour. In his yard sits a broken-down gold 1972
Pontiac LeMans and a rotting green 1973 Pontiac Firebird, tires flat,
sun-bleached, rusting away. The odd passersby stop and after a few
minutes of looking them over offer to buy them, but after a few minutes
of futile negotiating, they stomp out of the yard. My neighbour has at
least twenty-five stacked garbage cans, a dozen bald tires, countless
hubcaps, at least three barbeques, an assortment of shovels, rakes, sinks,
pails, chairs, tables, a broken snow blower, a bookcase covered by an old
green tarp, boxes of you-name-it, all stuffed into his life. There's also a
two-car garage. This he has down to an art. In one motion he opens the
garage door and tosses whatever he has into a wall of junk, slamming the
door down so the stuff won't spill out and bury him. Another neighbour
once asked me if I had ever been inside his house. When I answered no,
he looked down and shook his head slowly as though in mourning. I
remember when I first moved in, and Mr. Stuff asked me if I would hold
a ladder for him. I saw he had holes in the bottom of his shoes stuffed
with cardboard. Had he collected them too? I thought it odd knowing
he owned apartment buildings, but then again I have lived long enough
to know nothing should surprise me, because in this world there is always
something else, because there is always in this world always something
else, always because there is something else, because there is always,
always, there is always more stuff

Red Is a Poem

A poem for multiple voices: loud voices, soft voices, old voices, young voices, singing voices, crying voices, voices that shout, voices that whisper, her voice, his voice, above all your voice.

Red is a poem just out of reach
Red is a splash of blood in the snow
   Red is putting down tobacco for a fresh kill
      Red is the smell of frying moose meat
         Red is the dribble sopped up with bannock
Red is a poem just out of reach
Red is your uncle drinking himself to death
   Red is his nose
      Red is your auntie sewing you new moccasins
      Red is being proud of them
Red is a poem just out of reach
Red is not thinking the Washington Redskins are tradition
   Red is George Armstrong, captain of the Toronto Maple Leafs
      Red is Norval Morrisseau's *Observations of the Astral World*
      Red is a one-way winter starlight tour
Red is a poem just out of reach
Red is Helen Betty Osborne (murdered)
   Red is Dudley George (murdered)
      Red is Tina Fontaine (murdered)
      Red is Louis Riel (murdered)
Red is a poem just out of reach
Red is the Beothuk (exterminated)
   Red is Christopher Columbus's sword (murderer)
      Red is President Andrew Jackson's rifle (murderer)
         Red is Duncan Campbell Scott's Indian policy (murderer)

Red is a poem just out of reach
Red is Prime Minister John A. Macdonald's greased palm
    Red is a country named Canada
        Red is a continent renamed America
           Red is a state as in a state of mind
Red is a poem just out of reach
Red is Mildred Bailey's big band voice
    Red is powwow, rock and jazz, hip and hop
        Red is cacophonous, melodious and unforgettable
           Red is a world beat/en to death
Red is a poem just out of reach
Red is learning to speak Ojibwe or Cree or Haida or Mi'kmaw or …
    Red is shame as in being shamed
        Red is racism as in being erased
           Red is denial (don't touch that dial)
Red is a poem just out of reach
Red is going to school and writing *Fuck Dick and Jane*
    Red is going to school and not speaking
        Red is a residential school's lock and key and no way out
           Red is Geronimo leading his people away to freedom
Red is a poem just out of reach
Red is N. Scott Momaday's *House Made of Dawn*
    Red is the dawn
        Red is Maria Campbell writing *Halfbreed*
           Red is Cher singing her '70s hit "Half-Breed" (Just kiddin')
Red is a poem just out of reach
Red is the proverbial apple and all that goes with it
    Red is learning to see red (not rose-coloured)
        Red is learning to be red
           Red is a sweetgrass prayer
Red is a poem just out of reach

The Poet

The commissioners arrive with a trunk of crisp new bills and presents and papers to sign and a bible and a British flag and a good suit of clothes for each to look impressive, and a Royal Canadian Mounted Police officer in a red tunic, and government words and more government words you only half understand because they call you an interpreter but you are really a poet who makes up stories as you go along, and besides half the words they tell you don't translate, and times are hard, and though you do appreciate the gravity of it all, it's a job, and you are getting paid, and they tell you everything to say because they don't let you see the treaty anyway, and besides it's been a long hard journey and you are fed up with these pompous white men, who tell you if the Indians want to stay on the land then tell them they can stay on the land, and if the Indians want to hunt and fish tell them they can hunt and fish, and if the Indians want control of who comes into their territories tell them they will have control of who comes into their territories, and if the Indians want protection for the future generations tell them they will have protection for the future generations, the thing is to get the paper signed, get the money and presents distributed and make everybody happy, and then get the hell out of there and back home to the wife and children, and besides you've got one eye on the changing weather and there's a storm brewing and the size of the water you're navigating in the canoe is an ocean, and you're guiding these useless Ottawa men who fancy themselves adventurers and soul savers but who really have no idea of where they are and what it took to get them here, who talk and talk about what they call expediency, and if everyone is happy then you're happy and expedend too, you think.

Treaty No. 1

ARTICLES OF A TREATY made and concluded ... snaidnI fo sebirT Swampy
Cre dna Chippewa eht dna, trap eno eht fo, eriuqsE, nospmiS .M ssymeW,
Commissioner reH yb dnalerI dna niatirB taerG fo neeuQ eht Majesty
Gracious tsoM reH neewteb, eno-ytneves dna derdnuh thgie dnasuoht eno
droL ruO fo raey eht ni tsuguA fo yad driht siht.

Benevolence dna ytnuob s'ytsejaM reH morf year yb year receive dna nopu
tnuoc ot era yeht ecnawolla tahw fo derussa eb dna wonk yam yeht taht dna,
ytsejaM reHdna meht neewteb goodwill dna peace eb yam ereht taht os
meht htiwstnemegnarra dna treaty a ekam ot dna, tcart dias eht gnitibahni
stcejbus naidnI reh fo otereht consent eht niatbo ot dna, denoitnem
retfaniereh sa debircsed dna dednuob yrtnuoc fo tcart a immigration dna
settlement ot pu open ot Majesty reH fo erised eht si ti taht renoissimmoC
dias Majesty's Her yb informed dna notified neeb evah snaidnI dias eht
saerehw dna, rehto eht fo snaidnI dias eht ot dna, trap eno eht fo, ytsejaM
suoicarG tsoM reH ot tseretni fo srettam niatrec nopu etarebiled ot, yrraG
troF rewoL dellac esiwrehto, enotS troF eht ta gniteem a ta denevnoc neeb
renoissimmoC dias eht yb edam tnemtnioppa na ot tnausrup have country
dias eht inhabiting Indians eht all saerehw.

. . . River Winnipeg eht no dnal hcum os, feihC eht si Ka-ke-ka-penais
hcihw fo snaidnI eht fo esu eht rof dna; ... yas ot si taht, stimil gniwollof eht
nihtiw dedulcni lands eht all forever srosseccus dna Queen eht Majesty reH
ot pu dleiy dna surrender, release, cede, ybereh od denifed dna debircsed
retfaniereh tcirtsid eht gnitibahni snaidnI eht rehto lla dna snaidnI fo
sebirT Swampy Cree dna Chippewa eht.

Detneserper ereh sdnab eht ot gnignoleb dlihc dna namow, nam naidnI
hcae rof dollars three fo present a meht sekam, renoissimmoC reH hguorht,
ybereh ehs.

Cash in . . . esiwrehto ro, laertnoM ni price cost current eht ta, spart ro
eniwt,) sruoloc detrossa (stnirp, clothing, blankets fo eriuqer llahs snaidnI
eht sa selcitra hcus ni edam eb ot payment hcus, ylimaf rellams ro regral
a rof noitroporp ekil ni ro, ycnerruc Canadian dollars fifteen fo sum eht
snosrep five fo family naidnI hcae ot yap, sevreser evitcepser rieht raen ro
ta dna Indians eht ot notified ylud eb ot, treaty siht fo noitucexe eht retfa
elbissop sa noos sa, llahs Commissioner s'ytsejaM reH . . . .evreser hcae no
loohcs a niatniam ot seerga ytsejaM reH, rehtruf dna.

Subjects rehto ro white Majesty's reH fo snosrep eht tselom yaw yna ni
ro property eht htiw interfer ot not dna, stcejbus etihw s'ytsejaM reH dna
sevlesmeht neewteb peace lauteprep niatniam ot dna treaty siht evresbo
ot strictly elpoep rieht dna sevlesmeht pledge and bind ybereh od Chiefs
undersigned eht dna.

IN WITNESS THEREOF, Her Majesty's dias Commissioner dna eht dias
Chiefs deman evoba tsrif niereh raey dna yad siht, yrraG troF rewoL ta laes
dna hand rieht tes dna debircsbus otnuereh evah.

Signed, sealed neeb gnivah emas eht, fo ecneserp eht ni dereviled dna tsrif
read dna explained:

WEMYSS M. SIMPSON, [L.S.] Indian Commissioner,
ADAMS G. ARCHIBALD, Lieut.-Gov. of Man. and N.W. Territories.
JAMES MCKAY, P.L.C. MIS-KOO-KEE-NEW, or RED EAGLE
(HENRY PRINCE), his x mark. . . .
[I mean what does x really mean?]

Wallace Stevens's Memory

In a pub down the road from the village of Criccieth,
the farmers looked me over suspiciously until
I opened my mouth and ordered a pint of Cwtch
and they understood that I am not English.

They continued their conversation in Welsh
and ignored me, more or less. I carried a book
by Wallace Stevens and turned to the last poem
called "A Mythology Reflects Its Region"

in which he laments in a last gasp that "Here
in Connecticut, we never lived in a time when mythology
was possible." It was a line that signalled absolute
forgetting, and it made me want to weep into my drink

for the Mohegan, Mahican, Minisink, Nipmuc,
Pequote, Quiripi, as Stevens's gold-feathered bird
in the broad-leafed palm at the end of a manicured
lawn sang of a life emptied of life.

Carrier Woman

I met a woman once who drove an old car
over a mountain to go to school. She said
she wanted to do something with her life.
Once coming over on a winter morning
she almost slid off the icy road.
Her story was one of survival
with some luck and laughter
thrown in for good measure.
I marvelled and wondered about her
and all the things
she didn't say.

In the old days a Dakelh woman
carried her husband's ashes for one year.
A sack tied with a gut cord slung on her back.
The weight of grief always upon her.
Each knot of muscle a keen remembrance.
Whether in the midst of sleep
or journey, the Carrier woman held her sorrow closely
to be sent finally on the wind
in a breath of release.
Mourning given
over to the other side.

I was thinking about the old ways
when we met. I am like that sometimes.
For a while we stayed in touch
and then like two feathers
we both got blown into the rhythm
of our own lives.
I still think of her though when the sky is right:
who is filling her life

who might have filled it
if she married
if she buried
if she carried that burden.

Why Don't You Write?

In the same bleeding hands I use to peel back memory, I held
an old leather postcard. Embossed on the front was a grinning Indian
sprawled out clutching a whisky bottle, the stereotypical bulbous nose
and goofy face. The caption above him in red ink innocently asked,
Why Don't You Write? I thought about this, and it made me wonder

if Uncle Why-Don't-You-Write even spoke English – what language
would I need to reach him? What was evident from looking at him was
he wasn't going anywhere anytime soon. I figured I had time, and so
I made a stab at it. Gigoshkoz ina, I said slowly in my broken Ojibwe.
But Uncle Postcard didn't answer. Maybe I didn't have it right?

Maybe I had the wrong language? Then it occurred to me, maybe
he just didn't want to get up? Maybe he'd lost his will to live?
Maybe he wanted to go quietly into that good night? If I left him
alone I figured he'd probably just roll over and turn his back on me.
It was obvious he'd been alone for a long time. I decided to try

another approach: Where do you come from, Uncle? I asked this
in the most sympathetic voice I could muster without sounding
weepy. Did someone buy you while on vacation? Did they stop
for gas at a roadside convenience? Did they think you were nothing
more than an innocent joke? It occurred to me that my questions might

be embarrassing. I flipped the card over and read aloud the name
and address of the recipient. Maybe I could conjure her presence?
Lily Hampton, Lachute, QC, P2. I could guess the approximate date
by the King George penny stamp, issued in 1950. I wondered how
Lily reacted when she got the postcard – did she laugh?

Nearly a century later, I could feel Lily's ignorance enter the room like absence, like cancer, and drill down to the bone. The wet pulp of shame and regret I am still trying to cut out of me after nearly a lifetime. Her impossibility of feeling Uncle Why-Don't-You-Write standing beside her with his little nephew staring up at her.

Missing

he carefully unwraps
the auntie he never knew
he sees her at nineteen
wearing a pink beret
and red lipstick
smiling
as though she had a future
she doesn't
she rides The Canadian
from the city
back to her village
to see her mother one
last time and ends
up walking the dirt road
sleeping at a cousin's
they whisper she's
been on the street
she whispers she's dying
he whispers he wishes
he had known her sorrow

Lake Cousin

When my cousin died a few years after being released from prison
I lived with it for years, what I hadn't done, what I might have done.
Then I moved unexpectedly to Kingston and lived in the shadow
of the very walls that held him. One night not long after my arrival
I wrote a dream: Inside, he discovered he could stand in one spot
and soak up the thinnest heat of memory of a family in a village
beside a lake fading the way of a bruise, sorrow bleeding into anger.
He learned to read with a passion and found the old stories the best
and though he hated the whiteness he believed had taken everything
he loved, he thought Shakespeare had the right idea, the future foretold
by a witch. By then he knew he would never get out, and even when he
did get out, the prediction came true. He died in unseasonable weather,
an unseasonable death, that even his new wife could not have foretold.

Under Construction

Terra nullius. As in empty.
As in emptied. Drained like a marsh –
think of Lawren Harris's *Beaver Swamp*.
Only landscapes allowed.
Not a bird or a bee.
Not you. Not me. Nothing.
Anybody can see to make the link or think,
there's Indians in them there hills.
Gone. Void. Vacated.
As in some New Age dream-catcher boutique,
candles, pendants, chimes
and incense all from India.

Take Ouimet Canyon, it used to have an Anishnaabek name
but Indian names are incomprehensible
and therefore, I suppose, useless
so it was renamed after Joseph-Alderic Ouimet
(Canadian Minister of Public Works, 1892–1896).
Bottom line: Indigenous peoples can be dispensed of
in more ways than one.
Block a narrative.
Map a country.
Build a road.
Claim a country.

Northeast of Thunder Bay
in the heart of Anishnaabek country
a woman in a convenience store
looks over my government-issue Indian Status Card,
looks me over
and furrows her brow.
She obviously thinks I'm *white*.

Later I look in the car mirror
and discover I do look white. Damn,
I gotta get more sun.
I think maybe I should pull a Grey Owl
and buy a tanning machine
or join a spa. Get thee to a pharmacy
for some colour! Construct yourself.
De/con/struct yourself.

At Ouimet the land falls one hundred metres beneath my feet.
I step over the edge of the canyon
and fly into a cool moist bed
of arctic plants
    (found normally a thousand kilometres away)
a gorge cut into Lake Superior's north shore
by the power of wind, rain and story.
I spot a brass plaque.
    (Is this what it's come down to? A few words
    on a plaque.)
It says something like this:

    Once a young man (anonymous like most Indians)
    whom everyone thought good and honourable
    wooed the trickster Nanabush's[2] daughter Winona.
    Then one day while he was clearing rock
    from the bottom of He-Met-Her-There-Canyon
    he accidently dropped a stone upon her
    and killed her. Afraid of Nanabush's wrath
    he hid her body under a pile of stone.
    Nanabush searched for days
    until he finally found his daughter's body.
    Broken-hearted and disappointed
    at the youth's callousness,

---

2 Nanabush or Nanabozhoo, the Anishinaabe trickster spirit.

Nanabush turned the young man into stone
whose profile can be seen today (–
    by those who want to see
    what the land really means, postscript).

Back in my car I am fused to the steering wheel,
the road end to end tractor-trailers
melting the pavement.
We pass more road under construction,
enough gravel spilled to bury Nanabush's daughter.
Then another monster truck rushes past
kicking up a stone that blasts off the windshield,
cutting an egg-sized hole into the glass
at exactly the height of my partner's head.
The shock takes all day to seep into us,
and she wakes in the middle of the night shaking.

A trucker once told me that everything
we eat and wear, from a jar of mustard
to a pair of pants, the things we never think about,
they are all carried on a truck.
I don't know if this is true,
or half true, but it does raise an essential question:
When are we going to shop buying
all this shit? Game Boy this.
Game Girl that. LCD. DCL. CDL.

Everything a hymn to something under construction,
something big, bigger, biggest, best,
like this slab of endless ass-fault
or assault (now that I think about it)
pitted with holes and washouts
where we sit for hours
while the highway's tight pants

pinches my balls
or your ass,
and there is absolutely nothing we can do about it,
except squirm,
and dream of stripping down to our underwear,
strip it all way,
stark naked,
laid bare.
Where are we anyway?
What happened?
Go ahead, try and figure out what the hell is going on.
Because up ahead a jackhammer is pounding
your brain to smithereens.

At My Great-Grandfather's Cabin

After four days of paddling in rain I landed
among bracken, milkweed, nettle, alder.
Where the shoreline met the water
the cabin leaned like a bent, old elder.

Plank door askew, hinges rusted,
floorboards pulpy, I cut the cobwebs
with my hands and entered.
There I stood in the dull light,

and in my yellow raincoat
I imagined my arms wings, knowing
I was driven there by some almighty
force. What was it?

Then time ruptured revealing
itself in loss as I looked to where the roof
caved in, and abundance too, as I held on
to a broken table to steady myself.

Artifice

After many false starts I return to the beginning. I was beginning to
sound too much like you. I remember the first and only time
we had dinner together. I loved your eccentricity, your black uniform,
your cool severity. I tried to memorize your style. To put it another
way you were city and I was country. The way you sat so straight
in the grand room in view of the baby grand while I hunched over
my plate wolfing my dinner down with my fingers. Someone cleared
his throat (your ex perhaps?) I looked up sheepishly and quickly
extracted my hands from my plate.

Nice, you said, when I showed you my poetry. I could tell what
you really thought: too local, too unbelievable, too confessional,
too sad. Did I hear the word *melodramatic* creep from your mouth?
You made a comment, asked if the present participle in the progressive
tense would be more effective. You always had such control. When I
said irately, what I write is not material, you smiled (cynically, if not
sardonically) and took my hand in yours. The next day we visited
the Musée des Beaux-Arts where you sat me down gently in front of
a Paul Kane. You thought yourself so clever. His portraits looked so
well-fed, so stoic in their complacency. They made you believe him.

Pauline Johnson's Dress, 1892

The first thing we notice is your hourglass waist, and we instinctively
open our hands as if to hold you, all of us wondering if you wore a corset,
the kind made of metal or bone designed to shape you into the perfect
exotic specimen.

Slight, we think, for a woman of your stature still standing on edge of
controversy. But we have to admit the buckskin dress you wore to
dramatize your recitals disappoints us. Stiff, faded, silver broaches
tarnished. Ermine trim yellowed, long dead. If it had eyes
they would be glass.

An accompanying performance poster features a daring young woman:

> Miss E. Pauline Johnson,
> In her Unique and Refined Recitals of Her Own Works.
> Canada's Foremost Comedienne and Poetess.
> Pathetic, Dramatic, Patriotic.
> Endorse and Applaud her.

But here we are, and there you are always on the hilt of separation. A play
on words and we're the ones bound to ask if your ability to arouse pity,
sympathy, sadness made you the riveting stage presence they say you
were, or did that old serpent of doubt crawl its way into you and truly
make you feel pitiful, pathetic?

Yes, here we are talking to ourselves in this sad twenty-first century,
projecting onto you as so many have done before, maybe we're the ones
feeling inadequate, miserable, poseurs, when you in fact were the real
thing, if such a thing exists. And what of love or should we dare ask? You
would probably just laugh it off or maybe feign the embarrassment of
your age.

A cordon of wire and over a hundred years separates us, my dear Pauline: there you are in that same dress, staring us down, arms bare, hands on hips, head tilted back, eyes flipping time. And here we are still trying to respond in the only way we know how.

At Père-Lachaise

Everything changes except my love,
writes Apollinaire. At his gravesite
the heavy sky opens and comes down
hard enough to tick-tock against
the granite tombs, where other tourists
try desperately to follow their maps
in the stone maze. How can we
not think of a moment in our lives
we all want to relive? To say sorry,
and bask in the indomitable light
of forgiveness. Who was that young man?
Who gave himself up to her and jumped
out of a second-floor window.

But we all know there is no chance
to make amends. The distance of a lifetime
will not allow it. We would only be foolish
in our loss. Besides a straight line
without variance in the end shortens
everything. My son plays by himself among
the countless graves, and I make sure
to keep an eye on him. He could easily
get lost in the grey afternoon. The rain
doesn't let up, and I decide to call it a day
in Paris, the wettest in 150 years.
Our loneliness temporarily assuaged
as we join hands and run for cover.

The Zen Garden in Kyoto

Notebook entry. December, Ginkaku-ji,
the Silver Pavilion. All day long
the monks work to pick stray leaves
from the raked sand garden
to set it right.
Like the wind, we foreigners
blow in, stare and admire,
upset the calm,
Mount Fuji in a mound of white sand
rippling through the universe.

The cold seeps into me as I roam the temple.
Brought to remembering my home
across the great pond
and the Japanese family living among us,
exiles from their own land,
who gave my childhood hands
seaweed cookies
tasting like an ocean
I had never seen.

The grey sky holds our breath
like the coming snow,
we speak in reverential tones
until we are out under it
and I reach to hold my frozen feet
offer my companions

a touch of Japan,
bare feet on a cypress floor,
winter through the toes,
a few hushed words to make us laugh,
while I think about how far I have come
and do my best to keep balance.

Lluvia De Oro

Here under ceiling fans circulating the warm Cuban winter,
I wonder what a revolution would look like back home,
but I find it impossible to even think such a thing.
Here among waiters in their formal black-and-white attire
dressed exactly like the dusty photographs on the wall,
we sit like the Canadian vacationers we are but don't really
want to be, but this is their country and history, and when I ask
about Indians they look at me as though I must be an anthropologist.
Long gone the way of the passenger pigeon, they shrug. And nothing
I ask or say will change that. No melancholy wanted tonight, I get
with an elbow to my ribs.

The mansion we are staying in is divided into a rooming house,
an ornate bed in the centre of our room, above it a modernist
painting, circa 1930. In the evening I lie in bed and stare at it,
everything turned on its head. If I could I would crawl inside
that moment and take a look around. See what it was like before
the revolution for the wealthy few – for the impoverished many.
See what drove them to it. What it took. All of it whirling
around me when the crumbling plaster knocks me back down
to earth, back to the blister I have from walking all day. Besides,
all I really want to do right now is drink my drink and listen
to the music about to start, played for tourists like me.

Fireflies

Never enough love, or too much of the wrong kind.
Pitiful things we were in the tall grass running
and stumbling near the stone bridge. Wawatasi,
my grandmother's name, becoming in an act of naming
rising from the earth, an act of acceptance and healing.

Not witness, supplicant, aspirant, participant. Not that,
the way the beads of light unexpectedly flitted above us,
around us and finally through us. To this day I have no
explanation, no muddled speculation, for what happened
that evening in Oklahoma, and if there is one,

it is beyond me. For a moment, wearing everything
that was lost and had to be let go.

Mississauga Golf Club

I was the writer, and I was there
to document it. They let me in,
and I stood outside myself
in the immaculate conception,
magnificent stone fireplace,
brass plaques, oak trim,
a wall of paintings – Indians
in loincloth launching canoes –
a wall of windows framing
the imaginary scene. Grand it was,
and I was there documenting
what was no more, a graveyard
beneath a building, a mission,
a school to teach the white man's
ways, a last gasp to save what
was taken anyway, all gone.

Hidden Residential School Graveyard

against forgetting, the atmosphere called for torrential rain, moss-black

earth-stone trunks of cedar birch pine spruce kilometres wide clinging to

each of us our limbs drooping green, thick and heavy and everybody one

direction inward towards each other, all of us alone in this generational

sidestep for the first time for many of us above ground forward backward

we thought no choice we chose NOW in debwewin truth in our mouths

mouthing silence in the overwhelmed, provoking bits of memory

sanctuary something akin to dawn at first light, hug smile warmth in

the chilly weather when all was all was us on side into ceremony inside

we passed unrecognizable even to ourselves, grace lifting us beyond

petty who we are, are not, wish we were, our hands carefully unknotting

moving into each pulse of family kinship friendship upon us like the

running, breath we all could hear in our blood, the drumming, the

singing, the rain stopped, our eyes gazed down upon the tiny graves

Haliburton Highlands Night

The car's headlights wrench open the night.
Trees caught in a frenzy, wipers slashing across
our eyes, straining to push the heavy rain.

Up ahead a tow truck and a man in an orange raincoat
waving us past the commotion on the road below,
a huge poplar snapped by the wind.

Up ahead a blue car crumpled like a tin can,
the front end suspended on cables, floating
above the ditch. And we, unable to help

or even turn around on the slick road, expect
more death around every bend, over every knoll,
and I think: How do you help the dead anyway?

They like to believe there were never any Indians
in these parts. It makes for a clear conscience.
It's not true, and the right thing to do would be to pray

and set out food for the spirits. But I am not travelling
in that direction tonight. Instead, I keep my mouth shut,
clutch the steering wheel and keep moving.

Old Warrior

Saturday afternoon I pick him up at the rooming house.
He catches me staring at his two pairs of spit-polished shoes –
one black, one brown – placed side by side under a bed
you can bounce a coin on. I take him to the Silver Dollar
for a glass of beer. He sits where the sunshine warms his face.
I buy the beer and he tells me stories. That's our deal.
I write things down. He smiles. He tells me about Korea.

The Patricias, 2nd Battalion, the Battle of Kapyong
against the Chinese where he saved some white guy
he never once talked to when some shrapnel went whizzing
through him like soft cheese. Says he jumped in and wrapped
a belt around his thigh and got him out of there.
Don't matter who's who when the shit's flying. He shakes
his head as if whipping the memory away and takes a sip.

He goes on about his ship landing in Vancouver where
he hopped a train back to Biscotasing, riding with local boys
through the mountains and across the prairies – beautiful,
he says with his eyes closed. The whole village turned out
at the station like it was a party. People he hadn't seen in years –
nobody thought he'd make it – and there he was all skin and bone
with the biggest I-told-you-so smile plastered on his face.

Indian Fare

Why is it in so many old B & W photographs there are always Indians
standing at some station? Suitcases. Packsacks. Boxes. Bags. Trunks.
Maybe heading to some Bay store or back into the bush, families going to
Biscotasing or Nemegos or Pogamasing or the bright lights of Chapleau,
furs exchanged for groceries and a mixed bag of sweets for the kids.
Could it be that since the invention of that perfect first birchbark canoe,
the parting of the first skies, coming of first rains rising and shifting
mountains, pouring a deluge of freshly carved rivers in a continent
called Great Turtle Island, the Anishinaabek have always loved to
travel?

*Ghosts everywhere. The CPR's indentured Chinese blasting their way across
the country. Trains full of red tunic Royal Mounted Police. Artillery. Canada
proudly flexing its fledgling nation muscle.*

At one-time Indian Fare meant riding The Canadian – coach, sleep in
the seat non-redeemable, non-transferable. Half the community waiting
on every train, two east and westbound every day whether they were
taking it or not. Like a brass band with instruments polished and ready
for a party, everybody cheerful in beaded conversation gossiping just
to be there to see who was getting off and on. A puff of smoke, a release
of steam, sigh of brakes, sigh of your seat as you sank into it, waving
goodbye, mouthing you'll be back tomorrow, someday, along with all
the other believers. Only half believing you made it. Full fare. Half fare.
Indian fare.

*Ghosts everywhere. The railroad carrying the get-rich speculators, deeds in
hand, waving them like the British flag. Possession, dispossession the order
of the day. (Careful not to soil their spit and polish boots.)*

Pay this or that fare. Except if you were a railroad family or knew the
conductor or engineer, lucky enough to sit up front in the engine rumble

or in the tail end caboose swaying with the pot-belly stove, the whisky-swigging card-playing son of a bitch brakeman. Kids racing the aisle of the coach like annoying pets. Lovers nestled up under the glass dome car, a canopy of stars swirling northern lights. Old-time elders, plaid shirts and skirts, hair oiled and pleated or cropped, caps tilted jauntily. Sharing a drink with the luggage and dogs, stories about how their trapline got confiscated and turned into a park or about hitting pay dirt and giving it all away to relatives, talking quietly about this, that and the other but never about The Schools that too private. Young women pressed to their glass reflection, anticipation, trepidation, hope, as night changed her clothes and tiny villages grow into one-street towns or brawling cities. Men sniffing out the bar car like hounds, strangers becoming best buddies over beer and talk of war. Talk of fist fights and blackouts conveniently omitted.

Ghosts everywhere. The railway both nemesis and companion, tearing apart communities, carrying hordes of settlers, the foot soldiers of colonization, and yet becoming a lifeline, travelling up and down the railroad a way of life.

Because this trip is all about feeling good, no talk about this very same railroad bulldozing them off the land, no, none of that – for now it's all about getting out and moving on. And, oh, the tin-can Budd Car shuttling its sad little self up and down the line. Pathetic loved beast flagged at nearly every siding waiting for a signal from the fast-talking freight trains to keep going. Bug-ridden passengers shuffling on, lugging everything from canoes to new wives and husbands. Sun melting the tin roof, creosote heat rising up through the floor and not enough money to buy a cold drink. Paper cups of tepid water the drink of no choice. Or the steam heat freezing at thirty below and everybody huddled over lukewarm coffee. But nobody complaining as long as they are on their way in the clickety-clack of the track, in the swing and sway of it. Because above all just to be on the train means having a ticket, means becoming a fare, like going to a fair, bidding farewell, fare-thee-well, faring well and treated fairly.

Ghosts everywhere. The CPR *now primarily a freight railroad. Its beaver logo a faded reminder of the fur trade. The grand stations mostly closed, torn down. Sullen ghosts wandering empty platforms.*

Terra Nullius Lingus[3]

To be or not to be terra nullius. To be or not to be human on terra nullius
Today or not today we stand together dis(re)membered in terra nullius

Gitksan Carrier Cree
Assiniboine Dakota Ais Alsea
Wyandot Adai Inuinnaqtun Lillooet
Beothuk Pentlatch Tsetsaut Slavey Haisla
Chimariko Kathlamet Iowa-Oto Yurok Nisga'a
Miluk Powhatan Calusa Wappo Chehalis Mohawk
Mohegan Mobilian Tutelo Etchemin Chitimacha Han
Biloxi Shinnecock Obispeño Atakapa Eyak Michif Piro
Nanticoke Karkin Pamlico Narragansett Heiltsuk Seneca
Mandan Hanis Klallam Cowlitz Kato Kitsai Tututni Cayuse
Yaquina Atsina Molala Barbareño Atsugewi Karankawa
Knwalhioqua-Clatskanie Kalapuyan Costanoan Tsetsa
Tillamook Ofo Natchez Cruzeño Esselen Squamish
Ventureño Umpqua Tsetsaut Athabaskan Oneida
Malecite-Passamaquoddy Takelma Mohawk
Apalachee Penobscot Potawatomi Ojibwe
Powhatan Beaver Tonkawa Yana
Bella Coola Cayuga Sarcee
Chilcotin Tlingit Tagish

To have or not to have be(ing)longing on terra nullius
Today in our let me bow my head in conjugation in our for our terra
nullius lingus:
indanama'etawaa – nindanama'etawaa – nidanama'etawaa –
odanama'etawaan – anama'etawaad – enama'etawaad –
anama'etaw

---

3 In North America, since 1600 at least fifty-two Indigenous languages have become extinct
while many others are threatened.

BOREAL INVESTIGATIVE

Treaty No. 5

ARTICLES OF A TREATY stnatibahni, snaidnI fo sebirt Swampy Cree dna Saulteaux eht dna . . . seirotirreT tsew-htroN eht dna abotinaM fo ecnivorP eht fo ronrevoG-tnanetueiL, sirroM rednaxelA Honourable eht Commissioners reH yb, dnalerI dna niatirB taerG fo "Queen eht Majesty suoicarG tsoM reH" neewteb, evif-ytneves dna derdnuh thgie dnasuoht eno droL ruO fo raey eht ni, rebmetpeS fo yad ht42 eht esuoH yawroN ta dna, rebmetpeS fo yad ht02 eht Beren's River ta dedulcnoc dna edam.

AND WHEREAS benevolence dna bounty Majesty's reH morf eviecer dna nopu tnuoc ot era yeht ecnawolla tahw fo derussa eb dna know yam yeht taht dna, ytsejaM reH dna meht neewteb lliw doog dna ecaep eb yam ereht that os, meht htiw egnarra dna ytaert a ekam ot dna, tcart dias eht gnitibahni stcejbus naidnI reH fo otereht consent eht niatbo ot dna, denoitnem retfaniereh sa debircsed dna dednuob yrtnuoc fo tcart a, teem mees yam ytsejaM Her ot sa purposes other hcus dna immigration, settlement rof pu nepo ot ytsejaM reH fo erised eht si ti taht srenoissimmoC mdias s'ytsejaM reH yb informed dna notified neeb evah Indians dias the.

....yas ot si taht, stimil gniwollof eht nihtiw dedulcni sdnal eht ot reveostahw segelivirp dna seltit, rights rieht all, ever rof successors Her dna neeuQ eht ytsejaM reH rof, Canada fo noinimoD eht fo Government eht ot pu dleiy dna rednerrus, release, cede yberieh od, denifed dna debircsed retfaniereh tcirtsid eht gnitibahni snaidnI eht rehto lla dna snaidnI fo sebirT eerC ypmawS dna xuaetluaS eht.

Forever successors Her dna, Queen eht ytsejaM reH ot emas eht dloh ot dna Evah oT; ssel ro erom emas eht eb, miles square thousand hundred one fo aera na gnicarbme, debircsed evoba senil eht nihtiw desirpmoc tcart eht.

Derreferp erofotereh smialc lla fo extinguishment ni, detneserper ereh
sdnab eht ot gnignoleb dlihc dna namow, each dollars five fo tneserp a meht
sekam, srenoissimmoC reH hguorht, ybereh ehS... yas ot si taht, gniwollof
rennam ni-seilimaf rellams ro regral rof noitroporp that ni ro, evif fo ylimaf
hcae rof acres sixty dna hundred one lla ni exceed not llahs sevreser hcus
lla dedivorp, adanaC fo noinimoD eht fo tnemnrevoG s'ytsejaM reH yb
meht rof htiw tlaed dna deretsinimda eb ot, snaidnI dias eht fo benefit eht
for reserves rehto dna, snaidnI dias eht yb detavitluc tneserp ta sdnal ot
dah gnieb respect eud, sdnal farming rof reserves edisa yal ot sekatrednu
dna agrees ybereh neeuQ eht ytsejaM reH dna.

Canada fo noinimoD eht fo tnemnrevoG dias reH yb, purposes other ro
lumbering, mining, settlement rof pu nekat ro deriuqer eb emit ot emit
morf yam sa stcart hcus gnitpecxe dna gnivas dna, Canada fo noinimoD
reH fo tnemnrevoG reH yb edam eb emit ot emit morf yam sa regulations
hcus ot tcejbus, debircsed erofebniereh sa surrendered tract eht tuohguorht
fishing dna hunting fo snoitacova rieht pursue ot right evah llahs agrees
rehtruf Majesty reh.

YaKcM semaJ Honourable eht yb explained dna read tsrif neeb gnivah...
witnesses gniwollof eht fo ecneserp ni deman nihtiw Chiefs eht yb dengis.

ALEX. MORRIS, L.G. [L.S.]   NAH-WE-KEE-SICK-QUAH-YASH,
JAMES MCKAY [L.S]   otherwise, JACOB BERENS, Chief,
THOS. HOWARD,   his x mark
A. G. JACKES, M.D.,   KAH-NAH-WAH-KEE-WEE-NIN,
    otherwise, ANYTOINE GOUIN, his
    x mark...
    [You must know by now what x means.]

Zhawenjigewin

Today I learned the word for kindness. A difficult word
to pronounce, it sounds like tumbling water, something
to float on the more you think about it, study it, parse it,
realize its many meanings. One is a way of being.

I take this to mean a way of living. Another meaning
signals inclusion, implying generosity, and I wondered
about this too. I thought it as an innate gift to be shared,
a human patrimony. For some reason this lead me home,

which leads me to ask, where is home? Is it the place
we live? The place we come from? The place we die?
Where would I go to find it? I searched a river,
a riverbank and ended up standing beside

the Kebsquasheshing, a boy running away, running back.
The answer drip, drip, dripped inside me, coursed
through me. What it tells me is that not to find it,
feel it in all its manifestations is to be lost, stingy,
greedy.

Luck

Today the waterfront is wrapped in clear plastic.
I search for another way to describe it.
The beach, the town dock, the diving boards,
the monkey bars, the old bandstand.
All of it is preserved in sunlight so bright
it shines a hole right through you.

That's me down there, all angle and reflection.
I have buried myself up to my neck in warm sand.
And I am looking at the sky that is the lake
and the lake hurts to look at it. Then I hear
a bell. People are shouting, but I am
too far away. All the kids go off running.

A friend's house is on fire and everyone is burned.
I will hear all about it tomorrow at school.
I know they know that bad things happen.
Good things happen too. Like when you find
a dollar or something even more precious
like an ear or an eye, and there is no one
to claim it except you, and it tells you things,
shows you things, teaches you to beware.

Biblical

The scene begins to roll

grainy and silent

when I least expect it.

A movie where the road

comes to an abrupt halt

where children wear short pants

but are not forever young.

That's me on the edge

of the yard, agape

in my childhood

filling with something

akin to biblical proportion

a storm of locusts

a pillar of salt

incomprehensible and

terrifyingly absolute.

There it is again

the black and white

dragging its splayed

hind legs, a half-body

screeching and clawing

its way across the dirt

trying to get home.

So loud I oddly cannot hear it.

Until an old neighbour

hurries over and looks

down in his knowing

then over to me where I stand

transfixed, trembling.

And uttering what can

only be a prayer

or a curse

he raises his shotgun

and blows the poor

cat's head off.

God

All day the wind has torn through the trees. Today I think it is the end
of the world, but I have felt this way before, and the world will still be
when we are gone. I woke up to rain last night and sat silently in
the dark listening to the scraping of branches. When I was a boy I fell
on a darning needle and it went straight through my hand. It was late,
and my mother bundled me up and took me to the doctor's home,
where she pounded on his front door. He arrived wearing a housecoat,
looked us over, an Indian woman with her stoic son, and ushered us in
to a side room where my mother held me as he injected my hand
with freezing and then pulled out the needle. That night
I slept in the front porch so my moaning wouldn't
wake up my brother. Around me were windows, and as I lay
on the couch delirious from the pain and the painkillers
I watched streaks of lightning illuminate the night while branches
moved over me like giant arms. When I awoke the next morning
I could have sworn I had met God and felt his embrace. I was
going to a Catholic school at the time and knew Christ's suffering
intimately so I suppose it makes sense. What still stands out
for me though is I found him in the trees.

Old House

The pictures on the stripped walls leave behind
their ghost imprint. At the funeral, the eulogy
slipped out of me. I found the words and thought
no more of it until I returned to you, old house,
and found myself rooted to the very spot I took
my first step. Nothing will ever again be the same.

Old house, with your boxcar walls, crooked windows,
sagging floor, leaking roof. Listen: I lay up half the night
listening to you storm and subside, and storm again,
carrying me to bottles and flying dishes, cracked skulls
and silence. Then the gust of birthday candles, fiddles
and guitars, and riotous laughter of all things.

It all comes so quickly, old house. Tell me how to hold
back the rising current, how to walk through your door,
and get on with it, as they say. Little me, there I am,
pushing myself into another day where I am both here
and there, like some kind of divining rod snapping awake,
jotting down things I can barely contain.

Family Time

As I write this I can hear the distant whistle of a train

Under the cool spring sun everything is melting. Tiny runlets
blaze light while I sit immobile and feel the morning peel me
like a piece of fruit, scalpel down under my skin to viscid
where all becomes clear as the day we knew he was mad,
mad, mad.

Railroad, the word presses me to capitalize it

We cringed with fear when he came off the road, and he found us
cowering, and ordered us to do something together as a family
like split wood. Hold the block steady with our tiny hands
as he swung the heavy axe with all his might and we were
swamped by total darkness.

The wind is blowing sound in my direction

For a while we thought we could escape by becoming birds
and flying away. We found out quick enough our path led us
straight into a brick wall where we crumpled into bone.
We even tried to burrow ourselves into the earth, but our tears
turned to flood water and we floated back to the surface.

It comes in a long wave and then goes dead

First Words

Those women who raised me, nourished me, the ones who loved
me and whom I loved before I knew the word *zaagidiwn, love,*
who held me as though I were a spring flower
and unfolded my tiny ears to all the laughter
and joy found in an ordinary day, all the loss
and sorrow found in an ordinary day,
who nourished me with their stories
so that I would not forget:

all flown away, past the eye of the sun looking down
upon us since the beginning, when we understood it
as a sign of sacrifice and pierced our flesh or spread
ourselves upon stone pyramids, past a kaleidoscope
of moons and planets and galaxies, gone
to the sacred place
we will all go
when we die.

These women whom I miss more than daylight itself, I write
this poem for them under the street lights of the city where
I have landed in the flicker of a neon storefront,
in the magnetic glare of television, in the sweep
of traffic headlights, in the softness
of a flickering candle –
for you, too,
I write this.

For you, too, my dear lonely, you who are busy stitching your own life
in a few exhausted gestures, a few fleeting moments, you
who look into the mirror of a flowing river and see two faces
staring back at you, the younger self who for a short time
was as beautiful as dawn, but you, too, have been

broken-hearted by the death of your friends
and relatives, the murdered and missing,
the loss of all those
you have loved.

In the early hours there is a sound. I fling open a door of words.
You awake in fright. Think there must be someone in the room,
realize you have been dreaming again, or rather someone
has been dreaming you, into being, and there you are
among the star people, those who bring the nourishment
of love and hope. It is in this spirit, in our common humanity,
in our kinship, I share these fragile pages with you,
so that we might all hold hands and walk barefoot
together in the damp grass, in the wonder of all
that is essential
and good.

Bimodegos, Going Through the Bush in Winter

Tonight, you don't think of the taking because there is more
in the trapline guideline lineage line to everything that is now
in the thing that has brought you here to this point of breath
to fingers to mouth steamed to thaw as you untie snowshoes
and kilometres collected along the great windswept lake
of chigikitchigami through land your family has lived beyond
memory's dull eyesight where snow rips at sight making you
head for shoreline axe in hand to set a simple shelter among
spruce boughs into lean-to snow packed into a tin pot a handful
of tea with night descending frozen as you wrap yourself in
an old three-star sleeping bag listen to howl of wolf, hoot
of owl, twitch of chipmunk, scurry of rabbit, as a story rises
in a gust of wind slipping into you to carry you up and beyond
into order, connection, into what was, is and will be, in
a moment of reprieve here in this, a snowflake pattern
melting in the palm of your hand in the glow of a small fire

Birds at Dawn
(after reading Ted Hughes' Crow)

A loud caw
A mouth cave
A dark hunger
A Mr. Crow
(in one of his not-so-lovely transformations)

The day an omelette breakfast.

A daddy and a mommy
A baby
A screaming as large as the morning
A decoyed ploy plot fresh as the egg
A lull a – good – bye

The nature of nature's give-and-take.

As frantic parents' acrobat
As they dive-bomb Mr. Crow
As the intruder
As the culprit
As the villain

The unceremonious ceremony.

Of accident
Of design
Of that same old brush
Of goodness
Of badness

Me and you, black/white, myth of two.

Spider and the Sun

She spins her web to save the world,
in a last gasp effort to catch the stolen sun.
The effort made she pulls it home
to earth to befall, and become:
over smoky skies and tainted oceans,
ultramarine, cerulean and cobalt blue.

Oh, grandmother spider, how did you
do it when all our efforts were in vain?
Bear, moose and elk replete with query
in their suits of brawn, an imploring refrain.
On eagle's back I took a ride, my dears,
cast my net and snared the blazing orb.
A glance, a shrug and onward without fear.

Aware, and unawares it goes, the storyteller
beckons, the one with ears aglow: go now
and learn this story, made best by lesson.

Catching Bees

In the yard of the haunted house, uncle broken-man
yells. His dark head hanging out the window.
I look up but try to ignore him.

Behind hedges the height of trees, entwined in a blaze
of yellow petals. Those of us brave enough
catch bees on sunny Saturdays,

snap jar lids over them, lock them behind glass,
hold their sting to our ears.
Some tire of the game

and let their captives loose, drop their jars and run.
Others forget or neglect and let
the busy sounds melt

inside behind the glass while others maliciously blow
smoke into the punctured lid,
tranquilize the buzzing cargo.

Everybody runs past the broken window, making fun
of the broken man who calls me out by name
and says we are the same.

Congregation

On a road trip to western Ontario, near Vermilion Bay, we check into the Bates Motel, okay not literally, but I swear there was something in the room because that night we turned on each other with the fury of two rabid dogs until we both ran for the door. What was it?

Thunder Bay. Beardmore. North.
Sky. Water. Spruce. Muskeg.
Then a hill and a tiny church
looking down on everything.
A sign propped up against
the front steps, little
more than a half-hearted
afterthought: St. Sylvester's
Roman Catholic Church,
Est. 1852.

We stop to take a closer look.
Notice the peeling turquoise trim,
the lifting roof,
the rotting foundation,
the whole building
like the graveyard's
lopsided markers.

We try the windows
but they are too high.
We try the door
but it's locked.
The day is hot
and we drive on.
Five minutes later
we pass a few houses
on a reserve.

On our return we passed an abandoned church and got out of the car.
Standing there I felt that in some way it connected back to what happened
in the motel room. Not in any direct way, they were hundreds of
kilometres apart, but in some tangential way. What was it?

Treaty Letter

In this country I turn to writing after all these years. In Canada we are all treaty people.

I had just moved to Ottawa and found an apartment in what is called Centretown, once the heart of the city before urban sprawl. My apartment was on the third floor in the rear of a stately brick house on a quiet, tree-lined street. I thought, perfect. One day I was talking to the landlord (what's the etymology of *landlord* anyway: lord of the land?) and learned that the area dated to the nineteenth century and had housed the city's countless civil servants. I also learned that where I was living had been the servants' quarters. The notion of employing domestics came to me in a small voice telling me to ask to see the grand living room with its stained glass windows overlooking what once had been an elegant garden. Maids. Butlers. Piano recitals. Poetry recitals. Crystal. Chandeliers. The accoutrements of Civilization (capital *C* here).

That is when it hit me. At the risk of sounding overly dramatic, I swear it was as if two polar opposites, two opposing forces, suddenly struck a resounding chord and came crashing down around me (like a setting of china perhaps. Did I forget to mention fine dining?). To say it all started to make sense in the pretext of a feeble explanation is an understatement. I had inadvertently landed in the nation's capital, that self-same town where decisions by ministers and assistant deputy ministers – though I could easily call them sinisters – of Indigenous Affairs (read Indian) are still being made – or not being made – on our behalf. I went to a file folder and retrieved an old letter I had copied from a document about the treaty negotiations in northern Ontario.

I had kept my great-great-grandfather's yellowed letter throughout all my years of moving around.

All of my old people who used to hunt
near here are in great need. The white trappers
have stolen all our beaver, so there is nothing left
for them to hunt, and they are too old to go anywhere
else. There are also about twenty old sick women,
invalids and orphans who are very badly off
and they all join me in asking you to help us.

Chief Sahquakegick, Lake Pogamasing,
Ontario, Canada, December 1884

*My pencilled scribbling, my marginalia – if I can call it that – was still
legible. Dramatic and angry as the colour of youth. (I include it now with
veiled anxiety.)*

Children die of hunger as their parents look on. Mothers wail and pull
their hair out by the handfuls. An old woman digs with her bare hands
for a few roots under a snowbank while her family, too weak to move,
wait for her. Without recourse Sahquakegick turns to paper and pen
and puts his faith in the Government of Canada. But his appeal lands
on a bureaucrat's desk and sinks to the bottom of some dark water. (Too
busy. Christmas festivities at the Club Royal?) No help comes. The CPR
continues to rake in the cash. The speculators continue to wheel and deal.
The profiteers continue to fill their pockets. Desperate whites continue to
flood the land looking for a better life. When a treaty commission does
arrive Sahquakegick's people will sign anything to stop the suffering.
They would trade the sky if they could and really the commissioners want
nothing less.

*And my friend, now with the passage of time I ask simply: What would you
do?*

Sudbury, Night

An inferno of molten rock
poured over the edge
of the world. Spilling light
through the starless dark
so fiery red and sun white,
we sat awed, amazed, fully.
Ice cream cones
dripping over our tiny hands.

Piled into a car and into big city
Sudbury
on a Saturday night.

Fixed, fixated, transfixed
like a deer caught blind in headlights.
The grey rock despair
around us, lost to the current
event. Until morning
when we awoke wide-eyed
ready to leave the mess
of cold slag and scarred land
for the comfort of the bush.

Ethic

The newspaper shows men the size of ants
hanging from scaffolding as the world's
biggest stack goes up brick by brick.
Proclaiming an end to Sudbury's infamous
reputation as the dead city of the north,
an end to Inco spewing its yellow poison
over the landscape, turning it coal-black.
It was only when we learned the term *acid
rain* and saw fish floating belly-up in lakes
hundreds of kilometres away that we knew
the death had not vanished into thin air
as eagerly announced, knew it would take
a new kind of thinking that was actually old,

truly ancient.

The Coming

That summer we woke morning
upon morning to witness
the spectacle unfold before us.
And let our boat drift,
fishing lines unattended,
dangling over the side,
waves rocking us in
our exquisite excitement.

Our heads titled up, way up,
we put our hands to shield eyes
against the rising dawn,
and waited for the coming.
As she guided her little one
with what I could only imagine
appropriate coaxing and prodding,
as he searched for his ability,
his confidence in the manoeuvre.

And, then, it was upon us,
and I looked at you, a son
who would inevitably say goodbye,
and you looked at me and smiled.
And we turned together
to the tiny eagle
plummeting before us,
never once veering,
never once breaking,
as he hit the lake's surface
and rose with a fish.

Small Defiance

Yesterday
    we did ceremony.
            We sat in a circle
        in what was
    once a great forest.
            Earlier that morning my son
                    climbed into a lone white pine.
            He was surprised
        when I encouraged him
            to go higher into the branches.
Not far the city
        hung in the distance
            trucks pulling rattling trailers.
Still we managed to forget
        where we were.
            It felt good. The day warm.
        The smell of sage
            rising from the fire
    carrying into our clothes
    for a while.
Later getting back on the road,
        I slipped back into
            my straitjacket.
    The white material
        tied my arms
            behind my back.
        I drove like that
            all the way home.

Structuralism

The fact is there are many things we do not say.
Like most I neither felt the inclination
nor necessity. I took my solace
in a neighbourhood playground
and contently watched the children
until one day I saw them playing
the part of temporary innocents
in a melodrama yet to be fully realized,
but nevertheless inevitable.
Sadly, I could go on and describe
their futile little bird dance
against a plastic backdrop
as iridescent as gasoline,
but I confess I do find it difficult
to speak such things, my findings
anyhow dulled to a patina
by their light.

The thing is I was different,
not me. I was detached, removed.
I was not implicated in their tenor.
I was I, just as you are you.
I stood separate in my knowledge,
in my determination,
my claim to difference.
I was more than a window
in a sixty-storey apartment tower.
But oh, those little innocents
they have done it with their laughter,
their sweet drinks, their little wants,

digging into their bags of chips,
unpeeling the cellophane from their candies,
waiting happily for their drive home,
eager to point to more little wants,
not a care in the world you made for them,
not a care in the world I helped you make,
them becoming us.

Once

The source flowed through him
and her and all, and all was clean,
abundant, nourishing, giving.
Streams, rivers, tributaries spreading
across the land, unencumbered life
building to a torrent, flowing magnificently,
fiercely travelling through shield
rock etched by fierce talons of power
spilling out to great lake and ocean.

He awoke in darkness, shivered.
The day was overcast. He stared out.
By now he knew all was no longer.
The uprooted reality of it made him want to cry
out. Instead he chose to write what he felt.
Like a fool, an uninitiated fool, he believed
time was of the essence and hurried to share
what he had written. It turned out his audience didn't
give a damn for suffocation: dam, dam, dam.

When he was lost to this kind of collision,
hunched over his desk pushing around little words
like little shards of glass at particular angles
reflecting truth and dare you see,
he saw they really didn't care
about anything that wasn't about themselves.
What they really wanted was a reflection
of their confusion. That's when it occurred to him,
maybe what he did was childish?
Old man. Old ideas. Old dreams.

Sentient

Between land and water so glassy
not a ripple to disturb what you see,
a plume of green tendril sweeps
across your legs like an invitation,
an invocation that awakens your body,
numb swimmer of absolute beginnings and endings.
           Into this morning you go naked
and clear to bedrock
propelled by a shard of beauty,
of what little is left after such a long drought. What is it
that cuts through you, through the exhausted surface
to a fourth dimension where fish,
                turtle, loon, serpent
mingle below a necklace of cottages,
and – lo and behold – sprout from your limbs,
your trepidation, disbelief, wonderment,
nothing less than a terrestrial gulp
the size of a lake as you continue
harder than ever
to swim on.

Water Lily Woman

Is this an introduction, a confession or a plea? This poem is adapted from a traditional Anishinaabe narrative, and over the years I have rewritten it many times, and what you see below is but one transformation. I encourage you to speak or write or better yet live your own variation, because there is a teaching here about falling in love with all that is animate. By this I mean the natural world, all that is not made by human hands.

In this story she left her home among the star people and sought the company of earth and earthly beings. At night the people looked to a sky shimmering with hope and desire, and they saw one star brighter than all the others. He too looked up, a young man still imagining who he might be, and at that moment, he felt a touch lighter than a feather, a touch that made him shudder and look over his shoulder to the hand he imagined was there. Was this destiny, absolution or purely a gift in a time before time? Night after night, the people gazed upon the stars and saw that one grew brighter as it grew closer.

I think of this story sometimes when it is late, and I am in a taxi speeding home from the airport, or the train station, as I do so often these days. My head ballooning with the ride as I gaze out the window to the darkness gliding along the roadside. I think too of our little home, the garden that provides for us, the trees that shelter us. Go, if you must, I hear her say, but return, as I do, always, in word, a call, my presence opening the door between us and holding her in the dream of life.

She was lonely in the sky, this star woman, in the labyrinth of distance, a birthmark upon her luminous skin she was bound to shed. And so she conjured a different life and set her sights on the brave young man who could no longer sleep at night, having felt her heartache brush his skin and bruise his heart. As the star woman moved closer and the night grew brighter, the people saw that the star took the shape of a bird, her full wings outstretched, descending from the night sky, her passion penetrating the dream world of the young man, who sank into a fitful sleep where he sweated and moaned, sinking deeper and deeper to the place of their joining.

I think of this too, after the taxi ride home, when we are sitting in the darkened yard under the spreading vines, the stars all but extinguished by the city, and I tell her of flying and landing in a country where I forget how to speak, forget the stories that make me who I am, and she looks at me like she doesn't understand. And I think of the star woman's language, how she might have spoken to him. The grace of her touch, his touch, as they dreamed themselves together, and she unfolded herself for him like the perfect flower she would become.

I want to stay as close as I am now to you, she whispered, these words poised on the tip of his tongue, as she pulled him towards her, grasped to fulfill her exquisite longing. I want always to be at your side and those of your people. For I love you all and your land of flowers and meadows, rivers and mountains. Yes, he answered, please stay, and always be at my side, make the nights sweet with your starry lips. What a surprise for the young brave, when he awoke to find his star woman had turned herself into a water lily.

But perhaps he should have expected it. Had not the young brave told his people that the star woman would live among them? Had they not rejoiced and brought her gifts of medicine and sweet herbs? The next night, she had told her lover to ask the elders, the wisest of the wise, where she should live and what form she should take while living amongst them. Let the maiden herself decide where she will be happiest, answered the elders. And star woman saw that the people themselves were happiest when living near the water, playing in it or travelling over it in their canoes. And so in the pre-dawn, hovering at the water's edge she turned herself into a lily. This way she reasoned she would always be at her lover's side and those of his people.

Had this been enough for him? I wonder as I watch my own lover go inside the house, as I turn to look up to the pale stars. She had fallen in love not solely with him, but with his people and the land. Her desire had been much larger than he ever imagined. From the frigid sky to the heat of his body, the heat of sun-warmed land. Not only had she opened herself like a flower before him, she actually became the object of love, the flower itself, a love supreme. Did he still crave her touch, the stroke of her damp skin, the beat of her heart as they lay exhausted side by side? Or was swimming or paddling among a bed of lilies as far as the eye could see enough for him to realize the gift she had given them all.

There is no answer to such an old story, a story on the cusp of memory, coming from the stars themselves, springing from the water itself, just as there is no one way to tell it. Like the water lily itself, delicate yet resilient, such a story lives in a place beyond time, rising to the surface of consciousness generation upon generation. A footstep, and I look back to the house to see her beckoning me inside, mouthing that it is bedtime, where we too will swim into each other's arms.

Nanabozhoo

On a perfect summer day we gather around the old man,
those of us turned blue by impending loss. He says there is
nothing to fear. He says it like an answer. He says the snow

and ice and wind have carried much away but everything
once thought dead is returning like spring. There are stories
faint as an echo that foretell of such things. At his bedside

I touch his hand, it feels like paper. He says his mind is
made up to go, but his body wants to hang on. It loves
the earth. There is nothing he can do anymore, neither
for himself nor his people, and he wants to cry.
He has stayed human.

On his mantel there are photographs, angled to illuminate
those he will leave, and yet not quite out of the glare, no matter
how he positions them. No one it seems is ever clear enough.

I wheel him outside for a cigarette. Expect him to say something
profound, but all he does is enjoy the smoke. He has already
given enough. When I finally say goodbye, he says, I'll be seeing you.

As though I'll see him tomorrow or the next day. Later, I think
he is referring to eternity. Walking the sunny street home,
I am freezing, and as a last resort I steal words to warm myself,
bits of our conversation, grabbed and remembered, made my own.
Think of Nanabozhoo who stole fire and brought it to humankind.

A Wise Man Once Told Me
for Wilfred Peltier

When the knock comes
to your door
you will not be there to answer it.
We have been undressing too long
it is time
to put our clothes back on.

You take the water that is still
and the water that flows
and all the things in the water
bring them back here
within you
where they belong.

You take the land
and the rocks, and the trees
and all those animals
and the insects
who live in those forests –
you bring all that back too
inside of you.

Then you take the birds
the air
the clouds
the stars, the sky
and the whole universe
that too belongs
inside of you.

And then we take all
of the people in the world
and every language
in the world
and bring that too back
inside of you –
where it rightfully belongs.
When you have done that
you will be fully clothed.

And each foot will know
exactly
where to fall
and you cannot make a mistake.
When the knock comes
to your door
you will be there
to answer it.

ACKNOWLEDGEMENTS

Heather and Alex always. A big thank you, chi-miigwech, to family, friends and acquaintances who have supported my writing over the years, and to Wolsak & Wynn (and Buckrider Books) for taking on my manuscript, and particularly to Noelle Allen, Paul Vermeersch and Ashley Hisson for being so supportive and attentive to detail. A thanks also goes to Robin Moon for design advice. As a teacher who is always reading and thinking about Indigenous literature and poetry in general, I would also like to acknowledge all those poets, especially Indigenous poets the world over, who continue to write and publish and defy the odds. Miigwech also to Mishiikenh, Onagottay and Maureen Buchanan at the Kingston Indigenous Languages Nest for helping me to think deeper about Anishinabemowin. On that note, any errors in employing the Ojibwe language are entirely my own. Lastly, this book could not have been written without the boreal shield country of northern Ontario, where I was born and raised. It seeps through it.

NOTES

Although this book covers many things, some only tangentially related to the treaties, it was the treaties that sealed the fate for Indigenous peoples and much of what has happened to Indigenous since can be traced directly back to them. One thing is abundantly clear: what was said and what was done were two entirely different things, and the results have been nothing less than catastrophic for Indigenous people. This is something I've thought about for a while, and it was on my mind when I wrote the much anthologized "Poem for Duncan Campbell Scott" back in the early '90s.

"Doctrine of Discovery" was inspired by an infestation of ants at a cottage friends had loaned me. I connected the experience to the doctrine because nothing I did stopped them from taking over the cottage. They came and they claimed everything they saw. Its companion piece of sorts, "Terra Nullius Lingus," illustrates what happened, and is still happening, as a result of the (still legally enforced) doctrine.

"Pink Mints," "The Shop" and "Luck," among other poems, are based on childhood events. I did sweep out the local theatre, I did cut through the train shops on my way to school, and I did often ride my bike down to the beach on sunny weekends, but with the passing of time other details of the period intruded, and so I reassembled them to get at the poetic truth of childhood experience.

"At My Great-Grandfather's Cabin," "Bimodegos, Going Through the Bush in Winter" and "The Coming," among other poems, are based on the time I spent in the bush in remote northern Ontario, which I still call home. I try to return as much as possible but so much has changed. Sadly, the land has been pillaged by multinational lumber companies, and there are few storytellers and speakers of the Indigenous languages left.

Writing "Missing," "Lake Cousin," "Family Time" and "Old House" brought me face to face with family histories and experiences that were difficult to excavate. How many of us have those proverbial ghosts in the family closet that nobody wants to talk about? For many Indigenous people our ghosts circle around us.

I grew up riding the train, hopping freights, and I wanted to bring the element of travel into the mix with poems like "Under Construction" and "Indian Fare" while exploring other ways of travel besides the physical. "Fireflies," for example, while set in Oklahoma, is really about spiritual growth gained from the natural world around us.

"Haliburton Highlands Night," "Treaty Letter" and of course "Wallace Stevens's Memory" address, in different ways, the destruction and erasure of Indigenous peoples; poems like "Raising a Boy" and "Small Defiance," however, illustrate that we are still here despite everything, and while much has been lost some things remain.

Identity has always been an issue for mixed bloods who are essentially bicultural. Poems like "#1: Red Space" and "#2: White Space" are my attempt to 'wade' into the theme. "A Wise Man Once Told Me" speaks to identity in a much broader sense; it was given to me by Wilfred Peltier of Wiikwemkoong, who received it from Dan Pine of Ketegaunseebee Garden River in the early 1970s, and written almost verbatim. That said, "Water Lily Woman" was inspired by reading an old collection of Ojibwe stories that I happened to come across. I believe that the old stories have to transform and be made relevant in today's world if they are to survive.

I have to say "Reckoning," "Torque Wrench" and "Structuralism" come from a deep place of worry. How do we keep going with all the pressures we face today whether social or environmental?

The poems excerpted directly from the treaties speak for themselves.

Versions of these poems appeared in the following chapbooks, journals and anthologies:

150+ Canada's History in Poetry, edited by Judy Gaudet, Acorn Press
Arc Poetry Magazine
The Best Canadian Poetry in English 2010, Tightrope Books
The Best Canadian Poetry in English 2016, Tightrope Books
The Best of the Best Canadian Poetry in English, Tenth Anniversary Edition, Tightrope Books
The Café Review
Canada's 150th: Who We Are, Where We Are and Where We Need to be Going, Artfest Ontario
Canadian Literature: A Quarterly of Criticism and Review
EVENT
Exile: The Literary Quarterly
GRANTA 141: Canada
Heute Sind Wir Hier/ We Are Here Today, vdL: Verlag, Germany
The Malahat Review
Prairie Fire
Rampike
Regreen: New Canadian Ecological Poetry, edited by Madhur Anand and Adam Dickinson, Your Scrivener Press
The Rusty Toque
Syphon 3.3, Modern Fuel Artist-Run Centre
Water Lily Woman, Textualis Press

ARMAND GARNET RUFFO's Ojibwe relations were signatories to the Robinson-Huron Treaty of 1850. His great-great-grandfather lobbied for inclusion of those left out of treaty in 1905 when the Government of Canada's economic policies were causing starvation amongst his people. Ruffo's publications include *Introduction to Indigenous Literary Criticism in Canada* (Broadview, 2015), *The Thunderbird Poems* (Harbour, 2015) and *Norval Morrisseau: Man Changing Into Thunderbird* (Douglas & McIntyre, 2014), a finalist for the Governor General's Literary Award for Non-fiction. He is currently the Queen's National Scholar in Indigenous Literature at Queen's University in Kingston.